PERSPECTIVES

Youth Anthology

a Project by Women Wonder Writers

PERSPECTIVES

Copyright © March 2015 by Women Wonder Writers

A WOMEN WONDER WRITERS BOOK
P.O. Box 1134
Riverside, CA 92502

Book cover design by Women Wonder Writers

Cover art by Judi Randolph, Women Wonder Writers

Printed in the United States of America

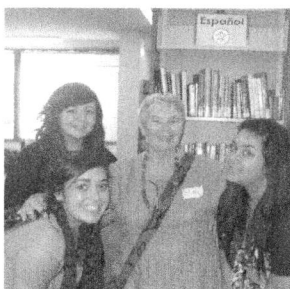

D e d i c a t i o n

for Ruth

Ruth Treeson, a hero who survived unspeakable evil only to go on and empower thousands through her message of love and resilience, was a phenomenal author, wife, mother and inspiration to all. Women Wonder Writers (WWW) had the honor of meeting Ruth in October of 2011 at the Laguna Beach Library's *American Woman of Pen Exhibit*. As a Holocaust survivor, Ruth fought to survive and maintain her core identity despite the hate that surrounded her. "To become a woman," she said, "I had to create my own journey to restore my life." After surviving Auschwitz and the murder of her entire family, Ruth found the courage to continue on, and as a teen, she traveled to America without knowing how to speak English. Despite overwhelming obstacles, she graduated college, became an author, and voice for millions.

Ruth shared her story of resilience and the power of imagination to our WWW youth, and inspired our instructors and mentors. Ruth's story resonated with youth because like her, they strive to rebuild their lives and let go of the past. She showed us that no matter what, we can always strive forward. Ruth exemplified acceptance and tolerance. Ruth passed away on November 23, 2013, the same day she was scheduled to be the guest of honor at WWW's Gala in Laguna Beach. Ruth will always be WWW's guest of honor and we remain firmly committed to carrying on Ruth's message of love, resilience, beauty of imagination, acceptance and tolerance.

CONTENTS

Acknowledgements

The writings contained within this anthology are from students who participated in Women Wonder Writers' (WWW) *The Write of Your L!fe* program since its inception in 2011, in collaboration with Inlandia Institute, California Baptist University Sociology and Forensic Psychology Programs, Riverside County Probation Department, Riverside County Office of Education, Riverside Unified School District, Southwest Juvenile Hall, Riverside District Attorney's Office, Youth Opportunity Center, Riverside County Sheriff Department, Moreno Valley Police Department, Path of Life Ministries, Riverside County Department of Mental Health, Riverside Youth Opportunity Center, and Operation SafeHouse. It is because of the support and collaboration of supporters and organizations from all walks of life within the private and public sectors that our work is possible and we thank everyone for their support over the past four years.

The artwork contained within this anthology including the cover art was created by WWW students under the direction of WWW Art Instructor and Riverside Artist Judi Randolph and Joan McCullough.

This anthology was edited in-part by Inlandia Institute Poet Laureate Gayle Brandeis and WWW's Publishing Committee Debra Postil, Elise Ferrell, and Wyvonia Brown.

Introduction

As I started to compile the works in this anthology, I was reminded of the many students contributing their work over the years since 2011, when Women Wonder Writers (WWW) piloted its first program *The Write of Your L!fe* in East Riverside. I have always admired the bravery of each student as they endeavor to express the ineffable through their writing and art. Their drive to create and share from their experiences through the caring guidance of our instructors and mentors has always inspired me. It reminds me how resilient each of our youth are in turning their hardships into opportunities to forgive, let go and move past the pain. It reminds me how altruistic our volunteers, staff and supporters are in making WWW's work possible. WWW has taught me, brought me, and left me with much more empathy and compassion than I knew was possible at the start of that first pilot program. Some of our early *The Write of Your L!fe* students have earned their associates degrees, gone on to college or trade schools, or returned back to volunteer and teach with WWW. Every day, our students inspire my and WWW's commitment to breaking the cycle of victimization and transforming our criminal justice system.

The poems and writings in this anthology come from the exercises completed in *The Write of Your L!fe* programs since 2011 through the guidance of WWW Instructors and Inlandia Literary Laureate Gayle Brandeis and volunteers. The students were asked to dig deeply inside themselves to explore what they want to let go of, who they were at their core or how they could stand up for themselves. The students shared different perspectives, exploring topics such as relationships, food, style and future. They wrote poems, journal entries, essays, quotes, open letters to (and in the voices of) bullies, victims, perpetrators, and future-selves, and letters to Holocaust survivors (who visited to share their stories). The students shared their own dreams and fears, views on respect, and the lessons they hoped to pass on to their next generation.

The title of the collection, cover art and art contained within this anthology comes from *Perspectives,* WWW's Youth Art Show exhibited in December 2014 at the Riverside Art Museum. The work was completed by WWW students under the direction of WWW Art Instructors Judi Randolph & Joan McCullough. *Perspectives* captures the various views drawn from our students' experiences. Most of these youth have dealt with challenges that children should never have to face, yet they persevere, show resilience and share their perspectives in hope others will learn from their stories. Expressing these things help the youth understand their past, but not let it define who they are or limit what their future holds. When youth are exposed to pain and hardship, it creates a burning desire within them to break free, get back up and keep going. By providing them with mentorship and tools to express themselves, WWW youth can shed the pain from their pasts to move forward and thrive.

The work contained within this anthology is published anonymously to protect the identity of our students, but I want to acknowledge each, thank them for their bravery and opening their minds and hearts to express difficult things; it is through their stories that they help others break free. I also want to thank all of the dedicated and passionate Instructors and Inlandia Literary Laureate Gayle Brandeis who helped our youth in their journey.

--Debra A. Postil
Co-Founder, Executive Director & Publishing Director
Women Wonder Writers

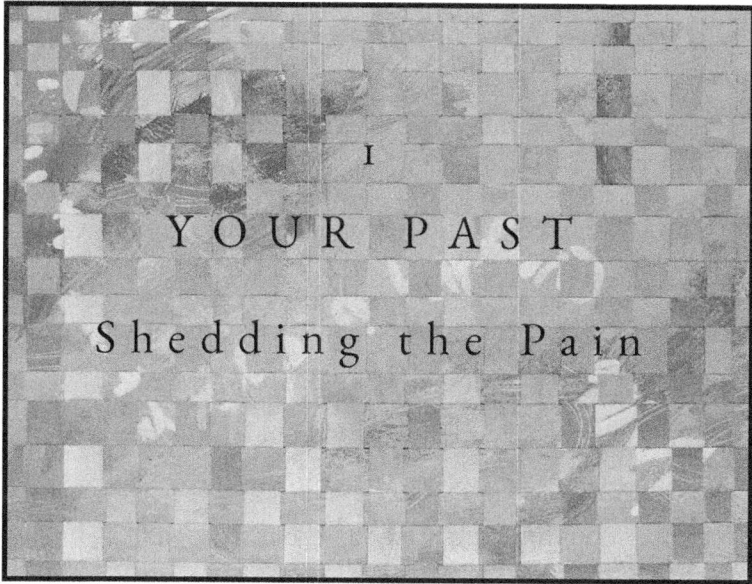

I

YOUR PAST

Shedding the Pain

The Past is the Past. El Pasado Es El Pasado.

I Want to Tie Balloons to My Insecurities

I want to tie balloons to my insecurities.
I want to set them free to rise and lift away.
And as they rise, I will be different and speak my mind.
I will say what I want and let my insecurities go.
I will finally be true to myself and not have a care in the world.
What if my hair is a mess or an outfit just isn't the best?
It simply couldn't matter less as I remember,
those who mind don't matter and those who matter don't mind.

Strawberry memories

Strawberries smell like the ocean breeze.
When I think about it, I wish the world smelled like that.
I remember when I was 5 years old, the strawberry reminds me of
my sweet and juicy escape from all the madness.

The color of a strawberry is blood red,
and that alone reminds me of the bad times.
The unripe part of the strawberry reminds me of bad times,
how my life was unfair, and how I couldn't make sense of it.

Happily Be

As she walks into the front door after school, there were things
only she knew. She knew objects would be thrown at her. She
knew names would be called at her. She knew pain would run to
greet her. She knew hard objects would be thrown at her; the ones
that explode in pain. This pain could not be worse than the hate in
her veins. The hate is the hardest part.

She knew she would scream to the top of her lungs. She knew that
nobody would stop it. She has gone through a lot. She will not let
it affect her schooling. She will not let it define her. She has no
friends to go to.

A brilliant mask of laughter and joy conceals the horror that is true.
But she is not all alone. There is one thing she has and that is her
books. She loves to read about happy things, magical things,
things of peace, and a faraway place where it is always safe.
When she reads, she too can feel that sort of happiness. She wears
that happiness on her mask for all to see. This is the happiness that
she swears and dares to someday be.

With her book in hand, she is always free.

Growing Up Fast

When I was just three years old and my sister was one year old, my dad came to the U.S. When I was five years old, I began to take care of my sister while my mom worked. I would go to the store by myself. I guess that is why I am so mature in many things, because I was forced to take such big responsibilities at such a young age.

When I was seven years old and my sister was five years old, my dad decided to bring us all to the U.S. We took two planes and one bus. I cried and cried the whole way. I was leaving behind my grandparents and friends for the man that was my father. I had no idea what to expect when I got here.

I got introduced to my cousins that lived here. They excluded me from everything, made fun of me, and picked on me. School was no different.

When I entered sixth grad we had just moved to Riverside. It was the worst year of my life. But if it wasn't for all those experiences, I wouldn't be who I am today.

I've learned that life is hard, maybe harder for some, but you have no choice but to keep on fighting.

Scars

Your scars are things to never be ashamed of.
They remind you of things in life you've been through.
And whether they're good or bad, they're stories
of bravery, weakness and lessons to teach
on how to be careful the next time on a bike.

This is My Story

She is responsible, caring, and has a passion for music. Her mother
got married and moved. It was one year into the marriage when the
mother and daughter didn't have confidence in each other. The
step-father drank almost every night. He would blast music at
midnight. The mother had three children. That summer the
daughter took classes in guitar, piano, and song. So every night
upon hearing the screams, she would take out her piano and play.
He would come into the rooms and stare at the children before
going to bed. Terrified. Violence. The mother and step-father
finally separated. It was a rough time. Yes, this is my story. I'm not
ashamed because thanks to this I got into music. I'm glad my mom
was there for me and so was my MUSIC.

Remembering the Good Parts

My strawberry was very red and beautiful,
smooth but hard,
It looks fragile, but it is not.
If enough pressure is added, it can be ruined…like me.
When I was little, my mom would cut up
strawberries for me and my sister.
She would add "lechera," a Mexican cream.
After my mom would cut them up, me and my sister
would sit down and eat them together.
It reminds me that even when we were younger, we were close.
And even though I had a tough childhood,
I remember the good parts.

Let It Be

The numbness that comes after the hellfire of words and whips.
Let it be. The loneliness that engulfs the constantly screaming
voices. Let it be. The shattered remains of one's own reflection.
Let it be. The craze of a vile angry world. One raindrop in an
ocean of pain. Let it be.

My Father?

Five years that I haven't seen you…And now the opportunity to visit you!

My birthday is coming up, all I asked for was to see you. My Mom was able to make my wish come true. I'm on the airplane, nervous to finally run to your arms. You didn't expect to see me all grown up. We both had tears running down our faces. Everything was good between us. It felt like old times. ..

I woke up in the middle of the night, with your arms around me and you are touching my face softy. I didn't take it as wrong. I was happy. Several days passed and you treated me differently. I don't know if it was the drugs. I started to feel uncomfortable around you. I woke daily to feeling your hands on my legs and arms. I would move and you would too but then you continued. I wanted to scream. You would bring girls to the house while you had a girlfriend. You would still try to touch me? You would still yell at me? Still hurt me?

I don't regret visiting you, I'm just confused. I needed to see you. I thought I needed you.

I don't.

Five years that I haven't seen him. I never thought my Father would do that to me.

She Watched

She watched
She learned
She watched Dad push Mom
She watched Mom cry
He did things
She never knew why?
Dad left

What remains?
Only the loveless lesson he left
HE LEFT

His Hero

The little boy cries
In front of a closed door
Sad, alone, and young
Made black and blue many nights
By those who did not do him right
He turned to the direction of the neighborhood park
Recognized from those many dark nights
The scene of what should bring happiness
His action figure, his favorite hero
Playing in the water,
"whoosh," "splash," "yay"
He saves the day
He runs and plays with his dear friend
To whom knows his pain
His best friend the action figure
He prays will save him some day
The bruises must go away

Misfits Paradise

Hide all your fears
Wipe away those tears
Cover up your scars
I am here
I don't mean you harm

Stand tall, be brave
Don't worry
Don't be afraid
Close your eyes one last time
Welcome to the misfits paradise

You're not alone
In this cruel twisted world
I'll be here
To help you conquer your fears

I'll always be there
When the world brings you down

Nightmare Junior High

Waking up every morning,
to a school full of hate,
Nothing but pure mourning,
for all that she has to face.

Hiding behind brick walls,
frightened and insecure.
Because they don't see
her as beautiful and pure.

Alone with no way to see,
blocked from those tears,
running down her cheeks.

Filled with resentment,
and scared with blows.
They don't know
what she endures,
everyday at home.

Even if she is attacked
with no remorse.
She has managed to learn to let it go.
Tears will fall and pain will grow

dreams have changed and destiny will flow.
 She won't give in,
She can't give up.
She knows someday,
Someone..
Will show her some love.

But till then they can see
her fall...
Watch her bleed...
and see her crawl.
Despite it all, she will stand tall.

Strawberry

There was a dent in my strawberry
It was abused by the hand that picked it from its growing place
It was dying of old age but smelled as fresh as a
Baby emerging from a bubble bath
My strawberry lived its life and died
In the hands of a toddler

Release

Release the hatred I have for a boy
that claims to be a man
who gave me a child
and he still runs wild
I hated you for leaving me alone
to raise this African child in a broken home
I release my anger because you gave
me love
love with a child that feels great and
lifts me above
I release you from my life
cutting this hatred with a knife

An About-Face

I am from a broken home, a home with no face where people are in their own daze. They have no life, no future. A home where the drugs didn't stop.

There was only blue, blue and red lights shine outside, a home that wasn't a home.

My home now is full of life as I lift my hands to Jesus Christ. The house with a face. The windows are so clear. The air is calming and so welcoming.

The blue and red lights have stopped.

Letting Go

My future self was telling me to behave.

It was also telling me to to let go of the bad

so there's room to receive all the good.

I feel as if I'm at the bottom of the sea,

rising up when I do all the good.

And when I do all the bad, it feels like anger

has picked up the world and dropped it on the sea.

Mom

It seems it's been so long since you told me
you loved me,
cared about me,
since you spoke to me.
To me, you gave up.
You couldn't try any more.
No longer did you care.
What's her kittens without a mother?
This is how I am, a poor little kitten
without her mommy.
One is selfish not to love her dear kittens.
It is a pity,
a disgrace to mankind.

May 23rd, 2005

I come from a big family that I love so much. We were all happy
and now it's not the same. We don't get together like we used to.
There's drama with some of our members. My mom died when I
was 10 years old. They killed her. Her birthday is April 23rd and
I can't even wish her Happy Birthday. I never lived with her, but I
need her now more than ever. My grandpa is sick and my grandma
is not here. I am not really happy at all. It is going to be eight
years since my mom died on May 23, 2005.

Ms. April's Impact

Ms. April worked hard for what she wanted to be in life. She is that kind of therapist that is always there for me. When I met April, I really wanted to get to know where she came from. Every person has a story and some people hold it back. Sometimes you need to just let it all go. Otherwise, you will never get over the pain and hurt you are going through. April has taught me a valuable lesson; when things get tough, just know that you can overcome any challenges God has given you. You just have to work hard at what you want to be in life. April has inspired me to become a therapist. Thank you April. You have changed my life.

Dear Ruth

I m so glad I met you. I'm also glad for you that you write books. You do a good job expressing your feelings. I like how you're not sad about what you feel, that you tell about how you can move on in your life, think of the positive in your life, and not the negative. I think you are a wonderful person. I am so glad that you survived the Holocaust. I think you were very brave. Thanks for meeting me. I enjoyed meeting you.

From,

Thankful

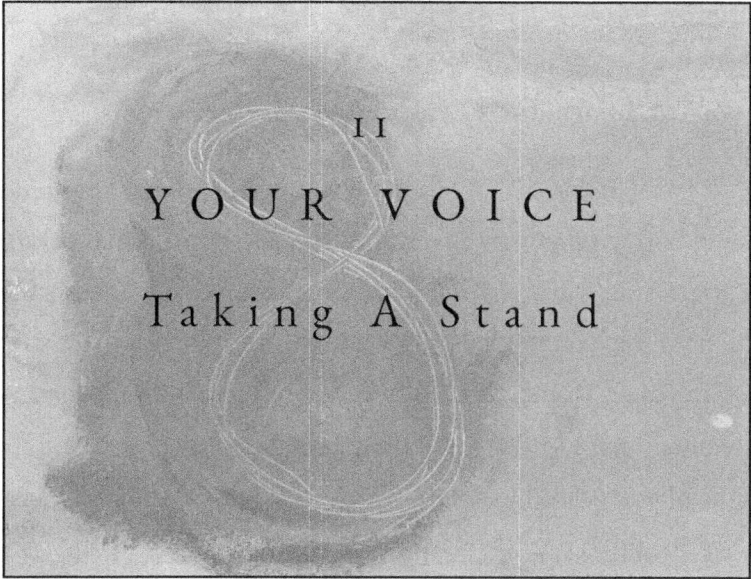

II

YOUR VOICE

Taking A Stand

Stand for what I think is right.

WWW Instructor's Perspective

This program was my chance to encourage, embrace, teach, and help young women. To my surprise these brave, strong, optimistic, fearless young women encouraged me, embraced me, taught me, and helped me! They all are so similar, yet so different. The young women are self motivating, inspirational, and strong women that I often forgot their age. Life has not passed them by; they have passed through life.

Oftentimes, situations we are given make us feel like our path has been chosen, dictated, and designed for us, bumps and all. The truth is we have a voice, we have a right, we have our words, we have our pen, and we have our RIGHT to be who we are, design our destiny, shape our path, and make our future. We are young, we are free, we are adventurous, we are warriors, we are Women Wonder Writers and this was the Write of our lives.

The Voice

It was telling me to behave and stuff.
But it was also telling me to let go of the bad,
so there's room to receive all the good.
I feel as if I'm at the bottom of the sea,
rising up when I do what is good.
And when I do what is bad, it feels like an anchor
picked the world and dropped it on the sea.

Imperfection

My strawberry has many seeds.
No seed seems to be the same.
Like no one is the same as you.
No one can tell you who to be or want to do.
A strawberry is small and prickly.
Some are perfect and some are not.
It reminds me that no one is perfect.
We all make mistakes.

The Rape

Rape. Nightmare. Trust and love destroyed.

This was her reality

She was just nine, a child.

Her uncle didn't care.

He wronged her in a rude, disrespectful way!

He touched her in a way he shouldn't dare.

She didn't tell. She didn't dare.

One day her mother left for work.

Her uncle was to watch over her.

Nobody knew what her uncle would do.

She was too afraid to say.

That day, that day, that day…

He raped her. He taped her. He further betrayed her.

Hate. Pain. Shame. Hate.

Her mother returned.

She couldn't tell. She wouldn't tell.

Life was hell.

Those years. Those years. Those years.

Castle of Fears.

She grew older.

She met a boy who became a best friend.

She told.

This boy stood up.

He helped her up

In an alley way, he confronted her rapist

He punished her rapist.

Her pain did not go away.

But, she learned there was a way.

He could be destroyed.

The weapon was to tell.

TELL!

Leave

Get away, pain in my heart. Leave and never come back! I don't
want or need you, but yet I still keep you. I don't understand it, but
I feel like you have always been there. You are a black
hole devouring anything good that tries to touch my heart, so go
and stay gone because all you are is a pain that keeps me down in
life. You're something I never talk about, because you hurt too
much. So leave me! Leave me so I can grow, so I can
love, so I can fill that empty black hole with something more than
you, my pain.

I Will Let Go

As of today I will let go of all my worries. I will not worry about someone who doesn't worry about me. As of today my worries aren't worries any more. I will let go no matter what it takes. As a matter of fact I already let go!

I can see my worries wandering around right before my eyes, fading away, begging me to let them back in. NEVER I say! I will not be unhappy for you anymore. I was at one point, but there is no point in it now because you never worried about me!

The Woman Inside Me

The woman inside me is screaming to get out.

She wants to tell me its okay to yell and shout.
To let out all my insecurities out.
But the outside me – the fake one – doesn't let her – won't let her.
For fear of feelings unknown, feelings like joy and happiness.
The woman inside me is not afraid and will come out someday.

Watermelon

Watermelon, watermelon.
If I had you, I would eat you up
and then get another and eat you.
Watermelon, watermelon.
Your juice is so good.
I love your seeds, because
you can spit them out.
Watermelon, watermelon.
You taste so good to me.
That's why I like you so very much.
Watermelon, watermelon.
You are so red.
Watermelon, watermelon.

Mangos

These mangos I eat
So soft and sweet.
They are hard to eat.
They are messy and they hurt my throat.
Mangos go with chili and lime.
These are mine with
Chili and lime.

The Calm Truth

Respect means people don't talk behind my back.

And I don't talk behind theirs.

I was mad at a girl once.

She talked behind my back to my roommate.

I got sad.

I understood that it doesn't matter what people say.

All that matters is that it is not true;

And that I respect myself and others.

I love the word Peace.

Peace means that everything should be calm.

It is so nice to be in this serenity.

When I'm mad at my mom,

I take deep breaths.

I calm myself.

Like roses that are red.

And violets that are blue.

Isn't that calm?

That is peace.

Nurturing Respect

Respect is like a tree.

It grows.

It falls.

Like a grade, you have to earn it.

But don't get too excited.

You can lose it.

When someone gives me respect,

I feel like a kid in a candy store.

Without enough money for the one candy bar I really want,

Some nice person gives me money.

It's more than I need.

I get so excited.

I feel so good inside.

Not all people are bad and mean.

There are some that are nice and care about me.

They know how I feel.

I learn to trust them.

I feel respected.

And I respect them.

Courage to Stand Up

Juan is gay and proud of it, but he lost his pride in the Eighth grade because of bullying. I think the education system should be changed to deal with bullying so kids like Juan won't lose their courage to stand up for themselves. Juan and I went to Elementary School together and we were really good friends. Juan came out of the closet when we were in the Eighth grade, but he only told a couple of friends that he was gay. One of those friends told everyone about him being gay. This left Juan feeling betrayed. He lost his courage to stand up. When other students found out about Juan being gay, he became shunned by everyone. A lot of his friends left his side because of pressure from other school kids.

Juan is just one example of how kids are subjected to bullying at school. I have been subjected to bullying all throughout elementary, middle school and now through high school. I don't want anyone else to go through what I or many others like Juan have gone through. High school is supposed to be fun for us teenagers, while we learn things we need to know. School is also supposed to be a safe environment. At this point it is not a safe place for many kids and teenagers. I've noticed a lot of things that could be changed about high school, but the number one thing that I think should change is how the education system addresses bullying. In high school, we should learn the importance of accepting one another for who we are.

The education system could have a program that is taught in class with fun lessons about the signs and effects of bullying. It could be part of our regular class. Speakers could come in and talk about how they were bullied. Juan can come back and share his story. I could share mine. We could write about bullying and talk about experiences we have in common. We could come up with ways to handle different situations. We could talk about race, gender, and homosexuality. We can learn to accept each other and have respect for one another.

If there had been a class on bullying back when Juan and I were in the Eighth grade, it might have been easier for Juan to come out of the closet without losing his pride and courage to stand up.

Stand Up To Abuse

The things I remember are my mom tucking me and my sisters into bed and then looking over at the man next to the door. I knew we were safe when he was there. Sitting at the foot of the door with a gun by his side.

I lived with all these men from the gang. They would lock up the house, do the yard, and make me food. They were very nice. I didn't quite understand why they were there, they just were. It was normal. My grandma would give them kisses on the cheek and say "Be careful" when they left the house. They were all like my uncles, protecting the house and my family. They were my family. They taught me to defend and fight for my own. They told me about the enemy. They told me to trust no one but your family and own kind.

I slowly remember them leaving, fading away. My mom told me they went to work, but, in reality, they were getting locked up and being killed. The last to go was my real uncle. We were sitting at a table in the back, just us two. Then I saw men dressed in black with guns out pointing at my uncle. They took him to jail. But before they did, he kneeled down and gave me a kiss on the forehead. He said, "I love you, mija, see you soon. Be good." I cried mostly because I had no idea what was going on.

Now my house gets raided about twice a month. I'm used to it. I grab the younger kids and put them in their rooms to watch a cartoon or something. My grandma still gets hysterical though. She's getting too old for this stuff.

Me, I try to stay out of trouble. It's hard. When I was younger, my sisters used to beat me up. Not to be mean, not because they were bored, but to teach me. When I would have gashes on my legs, blood from my nose and mouth, they wouldn't let me cry. If I cried, I was weak. I had to suck it up, clean myself up, then go eat dinner. Now when I fight, I now what I'm doing. I'm not weak. I used everything I've been taught. Some might say I'm a corrupted child. I don't agree.

When an old boyfriend of my mom's got out of prison, they got back together and moved into our apartment. At night I would wake up to her screams. He was pulling her hair, beating her. I wouldn't let a minute go by. I'd run to the room and tell him off. Hit him. Once I just went straight to the kitchen and got a knife, so he left that night. I said if he stayed, I would kill him. Another time my mom wanted to leave and he said if she stood up, he would break her jaw. I stood up and said, "Do something." He just walked to his room. My mom doesn't stand up for herself. She's still with him. And everyone knows he cheats on her.

I Am Not "Miss Ganglandia"

Some obstacles I have in my family are that we rarely have a stable house to live in, we barely have money for rent, and our lights get turned off every once in a while. My mom is a single mother.

My mom always tries to keep me and my siblings happy, and I love her for that. We all have different fathers.

My dad actually lives down the street from me. That is kind of good, but he rarely ever wants to see me because of his new girlfriend.

I think everything that goes on at my house affects what I do in the streets. I seem to fall for guys quickly, and want to give into their stupid words. I remember being with a guy just recently that said he loved me, but after seven months, he dumped me for his ex. Yeah, it hurt, but there's nothing I can do.

I think that some people can see or notice my fake smile I place on my face for the world to see. I hate how people think I'm going to jump into the gang just because my dad is from there. It irritates me. While I'm walking at school, some boys will yell out "Miss Ganglandia."

What's Behind the "W?"

The "W" holds great importance and significance; *Women*, *Wonder*, *Writer*, Work, Warrior, Wellness, Welcome, Wisdom, Willpower, Worldliness, Worth, Whistleblower and the greatest W of all, Words for they are our greatest tools and most powerful Weapons of all. When we are asking our students to write *Wonder*, we are asking them to expand their World view and seek the most out of life. *WWW* challenges every student to think, be critical, question, Work and demand more for themselves. Our curriculum is a call to arms to stomp out the indifference and ignorance plaguing our youth. With education, hard Work and critical thinking students can take on the World, never settle and demolish hurdles. We demand our students to have a voice, Write their story and own it. We recognize imagination is power and an unparalleled tool of resilience. It is with this combination of values and conviction that we build a solid foundation for our youth to thrive upon.

World, we ask you to take a stand find your voice, seek Wonder and get ready for *The Write of Your Life*™.

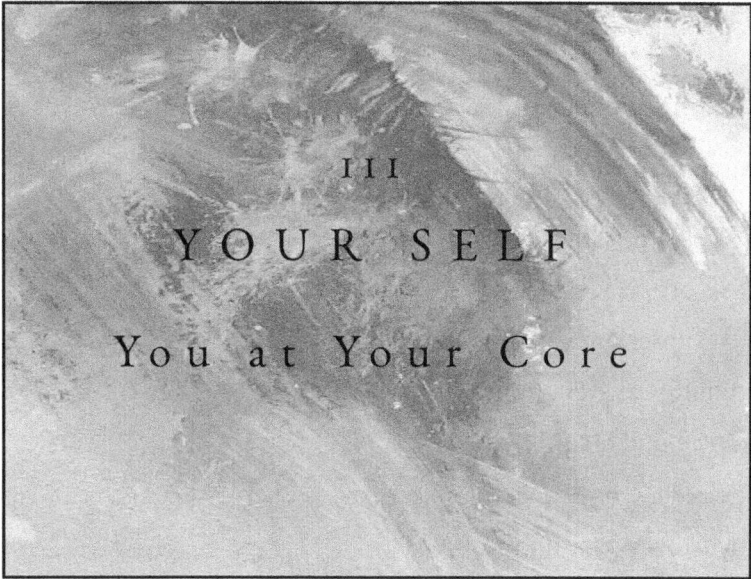

III

YOUR SELF

You at Your Core

I give myself permission to try.

Authentic Self

Mirror mirror on the wall,

Who am I after all?

Before life sets in

And pressures begin.

Family dysfunction.

Drug and alcohol consumption.

Violence on the street.

Mirror mirror on the wall

Show me my authentic self,

The best person of all.

The Others

Friends are like a box of chocolate. We have some we like and don't like. The ones we like we keep around. The others we don't acknowledge how good a friend they could be, until they are gone. Soon, the friends you like turn and you have nobody to run to. All you have is the others you don't like to comfort you and show you that someone cares. Then you realize the friends you like should have been the ones you didn't like and the ones you didn't like should have been the ones you liked.

The Real Me

When you call me fat, do not worry, I know it is you, not me, that has to change. I know I am beautiful just the way I am. I care less of what people think because I know and celebrate the real me. You may call me stupid, but I know I am intelligent and smart beyond my years. Look at my age and the way I expose my real self. I am me and I am proud. Hope; I like it, I want it and I have it. Hearts!

You Say

You say I'm worthless
and it hurts me inside,
but I keep my head held high
because I'm beautiful inside.

Broken girl

Undress her slowly, she won't mind.
It's the only way she'll feel loved for a few moments.
Touch her body so that maybe for a second she'll feel wanted.
Whisper sweet lies into her ear.
She'll surely believe every word.
Take advantage of this broken girl.

Bloom

I am like a rose, pretty and delicate.

But as you get to my stem and core,

I have thorns and walls to protect me from the outside world.

Only a select few get to watch me bloom,

because I fear, to open up to the whole world,

or a part of it, means to give up a part of me.

My only hope is that I can bloom, like all the other roses.

And remain true to me.

Peace & Respect

Respect to me is all about your inner self.

You get what you give.

Respect is being straight out with all the negativity to the side.

Show respect to others through just having a smile on your face
and being positive.

You show respect to people even if they disagree by just letting
them be.

Peace and respect is being calm and relaxed.

When disrespected, it's like a slap in the face.

Having respect for yourself is better.

Respect is big.

Disrespect is lame.

When You Call Me Ugly

When you call me ugly
I know I am beautiful just the way I am
You think I'm a slut
Go ahead
Say it all you want
As long as I know I'm a beautiful girl
Who knows who she really is
Deep inside

Dear Bully

Dear Bully,
You're wrong!
I know who I am
Smart, beautiful, and funny
You might not like that
But, it's because you're JEALOUS
Believe in yourself
You are wonderful too
I understand you
But, just know
You don't have to be a BULLY

Dear Victim

Dear Victim,
I know it was WRONG
You are beautiful, smart, and funny
I just wanted to feel the same

Dear Bully

Dear Bully,
You bully me
I don't bully you
I did nothing to you
You call me names
I believed them
But, now I realize
You're just a waste of my time
You're not my bully anymore
Because I won't let you
I'm better than that

Food

Food is art, a way
of expressing your self.

Food is a passion to
people who love to eat.

There's a theme behind food.

Food can be healthy
or bed for your health.

We the people wouldn't
be alive if it weren't for
food...

My last meal will be fish.
Fish are one of the first
foods when Our Heavenly Father
was on this here earth.

Blue Eyes

Blue eyes
Blue eyes
My best trait
Blue eyes
Blue eyes
Shiny and bright

Learn

Learn how to be yourself
let no one tell you something else.
Nothing's wrong with being weird
as long as in a good direction you step
And wash your nasty hands,
no five second rule when the food lands;
you can get sick or even die
and that would make your mother cry

Smiling Eyes

I like my smile and eyes
I think it's lovely
sometimes I just look
in the mirror and just
watch my self smile

and I like my eyes
because they're pretty
and my mom always told
told me that my eyes
tell a story, and it's
kinda the first thing people
notice.

Favorite Food

my favorite food is
tacos, it always has been
since I was a young kid
I love the way they crunch
and I love the way they
taste, they just brighten up
my day   mmmm.... tacos.

Strawberry Memories

Strawberries are
my favorite fruit
I love the redness
of it and the Juice
of it

it brings me back
to my childhood because
I used to love strawberry
everything, down to juice, chapstick,
lotion, and bathsoap

Music Lives

I would love to
teach myself how
to sing. Music is
my life, I listen
to it all day, every day
and when I hear my
favorite song, I always
think to myself *dang I
wish I could sing.*

Food

Chicken. Rosemary, Pepper & something special.
My favorite adult created art.
My favorite adult created life in my belly.
Chicken is good.

That Scar

There is this scar on my right knee; it all happened when I was on the way to the library with my siblings riding our bikes. It felt nice to have the breeze blowing in our faces; it seemed like a good day.

When all of a sudden BAM! I got hit by a car. I don't remember any of it - as if my memory was stolen. I had to have surgery because my bone snapped in half like a fragile twig. The pain I went through was ineffable!

That scar to me, means that I am STRONG.

Fruit

If I were a fruit I would be a coconut.

I am hard headed, stubborn and strong

like a coconut on the outside.

I am also filled with joy and love

just like the coconuts filled with juice.

My hair is like the coconuts, soft and rough.

The Woman Inside Me

The woman inside me will bloom like a flower in spring. She's full of excitement to come out, like a child's excitement when she arrives at Disneyland. She wants to roam the world freely like the wind.

Sometimes she bottles up all her anger until it finally overflows and explodes just like when you drop a soda and it would go BOOM and explode everywhere.

The woman inside me is strong like the Hulk and will, with time, come out.

If I Were A Fruit

I'm like a watermelon, hard headed on the outside

but sweet and tender on the inside;

containing many seeds representing many ideas

waiting to be grown and flourished.

Whether they are dark seeds or white seeds,

negative or positive, they'll eventually grow

and mature with time.

I Am From

I am from the garden where the flowers bloom and flourish every season.

I am from the empty jar of pickles piled up in a hidden closet.

I am from the playground where the bars were scalding hot during the summer sun.

I am from the place were trees growing tall and lean.

I am from the popsicle melting on the 4th of July.

I am from Orange County where it is inhabited by many people of many places.

The Woman Inside Me

The woman inside me is as sweet and tender as the grandmother
who would bake your goods. As intelligent and bright with ideas as
luminous as the man who invented the light bulb. The woman
inside me screams like the howling melancholy wind. But she
knows she is free as the ocean sea. That woman will someday be
me.

Embarrassment

The feeling of embarrassment running through my head,
that I followed my mom's footsteps. It was out of my control.
One thing is for sure, I felt like slicing my wrist,
so the embarrassment can stop running through my veins,
and it can be over with.

Giving to Receive Respect

Respect to me is all about your inner-self.

You get what you give.

Respect is being straight out,

With all the negativity to the side.

Show respect to others by just having a smile on your face;

And by being positive.

You show respect to people,

Even if they disagree,

By just letting them be.

Peace and respect is calm and relaxed.

Being disrespected feels like a slap in the face.

Having respect for yourself is best.

Respect is big.

Disrespect is lame.

Get what you give.

It's better to be respected than disrespected.

The Story in My Hair

Burnt, like I've been so many times

while angry and feeling the frustration rise within me.

Split, like when I've been torn away

from my family and not to be seen for so long.

Dyed, like I have to hide my identity

from the world and afraid to show the real me.

Cut, like a fresh beginning I've been offered in life,

like the new personality that's growing inside.

Layered, like the many steps I've taken to become who I am today.

I will forget the past,

but I will not forget what it has taught me.

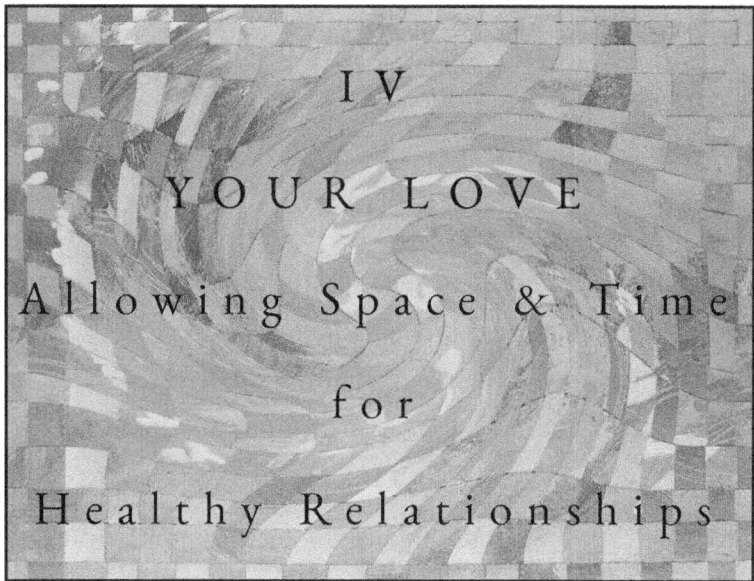

IV

YOUR LOVE

Allowing Space & Time

for

Healthy Relationships

In the silence, I understand that to love you must understand. To understand, you must listen.

Getting to Know You

Emerald is a dear friend of mine. People always want to know what it is like to be an actor, so I interviewed her. I learned many things about her that I did not know. It made me realize, you think you know somebody but you don't. There is always something new to learn about them everyday and if you just settle down for a couple of minutes and have serious conversation you become closer and learn things you didn't know before.

WWW Instructor Tips on Healthy Relationships:

Before you can truly love somebody else you MUST first love yourself.

Stop and think; how does this person make me feel about myself? Am I more confident around him or her? Do they make me feel special or insecure? Do they build me up or break me down? Point out my strengths or my faults? If they make you feel bad, DROP them!

You want the person you "choose" to love to enhance you by allowing you to shine. They should be your partner in that they are an equal and want the best for you. If you find somebody tearing you down, that is not a partner. The person you "choose" to be with should be your number one cheerleader!

Do not settle. Just because somebody may love you and want desperately to be with you does NOT mean that you should be with them. Choose who you want to be in a relationship with. A fear of being alone is not a reason to be in a relationship.

You are a complete person you do not need somebody else to complete you. Follow your gut. If you have a bad feeling it is there for a reason.

Do not ever let anybody hurt you physically or emotionally. If somebody has rage and either hurts you or destroys property that is abuse. Physical and emotional abuse can be equally traumatizing and are equally UNACCEPTABLE! Leave a situation when you see the first signs of abuse and encourage friends and family to do the same. Never keep it a secret. Most abuse starts out as a simple push or arm squeeze and grows form there in to bruises and much more- leave at the start!

Know your boundaries. Someone will never respect you more for going along with something- in fact the opposite will likely happen. Respect and love your body- so do NOT just give it away. Same with your heart.

Never lose yourself in anybody. If that person leaves you will find yourself not only devastated but lost and empty. There is nobody you cannot survive without. In dealing with a breakup or any rejection, PUT THINGS IN PERSPECTIVE! Take things one day at a time- focus on short term goals in terms of healing. You can get through today without him or her in your life- then start again each day.

Mark Twain said, *"Never allow someone to be your priority while allowing yourself to be their option."* It is true if somebody is one of your top priorities MAKE sure that you are one of their top priorities! You deserve nothing less!

There is nothing more *attractive* or *magnetic* than confidence.

Confidence will come from you finding your voice, knowing yourself and loving yourself!

Have You Ever!

Have you ever loved somebody so much it hurts?
Have you ever loved somebody so much that you can't sleep?
Have you ever loved somebody so much they don't know you exist?
Have you ever loved somebody so much, but they just don't feel the same?
Have you ever loved somebody that is in love with someone else?
Have you ever loved somebody who doesn't know you love them so very much?
Have you ever?

Failing Love

When love fails I cry all night and dream about all those good days
we had together. I think about your smile and your laugh, and how
you used to hold me. It still makes my heart jump.
The way you told me you love me makes my heart melt.

My Favorite Food

My favorite food is made by my mother. There's no other person
that puts the care and love that she does in every spoonful. The
taste of exotic spice and smell of freshly cut herbs, followed by a
warm and tingling feeling in my belly can never be matched by
any cook on earth.

Home

Home is a place I enjoy being
Not literally where I fall asleep every night and wake up every
morning
Home is a place where I'm surrounded by people I love and love
me in return
Not a house or a bed
Home is where I can be myself
Not feeling alone

Hands

These hands that are blessed with movement

These hands that are active and playful with my son

These hands that hold and comfort loved ones

These hands that wipe away the tears of the little one

These hands that my son will grow up in

These hands that will wrap around him and hold him

Feel For You

You say never do this, never do that,

but what's the difference?

You do it behind my back,

and in my face, breaking my heart.

Maybe you should listen to your own advice

before you break another heart.

As I sit with little to do, my mind is

filled with thoughts of you.

As I work hard through the day,

I will miss your smile that's miles away.

As I lay down to sleep, you must know this,

my love is true. I spend all my time

missing you.

Me

I want to teach myself
Not to run to people who drag me down.
It's like a game of tag
You keep chasing the people that drag you down
And eventually end up tagging them
And end up getting tired
But when you stop and think
And start doing the right thing
They stop running from you
And end up wanting to make
Better decisions that get us somewhere
You only live one life on earth
Live like it's your last time
Stop chasing and start living.

Farewell

I'm released from the nights I cried, with tears
In my eyes wondering if you were going to
Come and embrace me in your arms.
I am finally letting go of the moments
That you missed in my life
Because you weren't ready to be the father
I wanted you to be.

Family

Family to change the past
Wow a miracle
Family to start a new
The family of mine is conquering
My strength on making
My own choices
The words they say
How much they hurt
All they want it for me to burst
Family, is that what they
Call a family

Strawberries

Strawberry short cakes
A great way of remembering my grandpop.
Now we celebrate his birthday
With our own homemade strawberry short cakes.

R.I.P, Papa James

On my walls I would write love.

Safe Place

Not necessarily safe, but comfortable
If I wanted to relax I would be able to
In her arms smelling her breath
She is my life and I am hers
With her I am comfortable, she is safe

Trust & Learn

To be dependable is big.
Trust is even bigger.
Everyday we lose trust, everyday we gain.
Yet for me, I have built a wall of hate and unresponse.
From this, all I've done is push friends, family and boys
away so far that we stopped talking.
So don't be like me.
Don't build a wall.
Trust and learn from me.

Love Yourself

Learn to love.

Learn to trust.

Learn to be honest.

Learn to sew.

Learn to be happy and free.

Learn to conquer your fears.

Learn to survive in this world.

Learn to care for others.

Learn to be free from all the burdens in your heart.

But most of all, learn to love yourself.

Because when you love yourself

is when you can truly love others

and be open to learn anything.

They Only Exist in Books

My momma warned me not to fall in love with a guy like you, the
one who is shy, nice and cute.
The one who looks you in the eye and is honest.

She warned me that men like you only exist in fairy tales. And men
like you will only break my heart.

But here you are in my room. Your eyes hold compassion and are
not dark.

You give me faith that the tales were not all fake; making me
believe my life was not a mistake.

My Love

My love is like an ocean.
It goes down so deep.
My love is like a rose whose
beauty you can keep.
My love is like a river
that will never end.
My love is like a dove
with a beautiful message to send.
My love is like a song
That goes on forever.

The Right Way

Love is mysterious, nobody know what it is.
Everyone has their own interpretation.
When you feel loved you don't know how to explain it,
Or how to express the way you feel.
It just comes naturally, like breathing.
But only your heart is beating faster.
You can feel the blood rushing through your veins,
as your knees start trembling.
Hen you see them, you forget those words you have been
longing to let out.
So tell me, is there really a right way to express love?

Day by Day

Day by day I dream.
I dream I would never have to feel this pain.
I dream I would always have you.
I woke up and realized that my dreams
never come true. . .
I woke up and realized you are not always going to be there. . .
I can feel the pain.
I realized you aren't going to take me back. . .
I'm alone.
My love is what keeps me alive.

V

YOUR BODY

Perceptions & Taking

Care of Yourself

Tips on Healthy Body Image & Lifestyle

MOVE your BODY! You don't need to be crazy hitting the gym 24/7 or running marathons but you need to MOVE. Set a goal to do some type of exercise 20 minutes a day. May it be walking with a friend, jogging, sports or even jumping jacks in your room make a commitment to move!

There are plenty of exercises you can do without venturing outside of your room; sit-ups, lunges, stretching, weights, jogging in place, dancing, pacing while on the phone or even cleaning- be creative and make it fun!

Make moving a lifestyle! The more you exercise and move the more energy you will have! A lack of exercise can make you tired and thus kill your initiative to move. Try simple tricks such as taking the stairs, walking a longer route, rocking out to music…

Drink WATER! Water is amazing! It keeps us healthy through cleansing the body (helps us lose weight too). Dehydration can trick our mind in to thinking we are hungry when in reality we just need water. And NO soda does not count it needs to be plain water to hydrate! Dehydration causes fatigue and bloating - so hydrate! Water is also great for your skin, hair and lots more. Try to drink at least 2 liters (about 8 large glasses) of water a day. Make it a goal and count your water glasses!

Watch and know what you are eating! Do NOT deprive yourself of treats but take notice of what you are eating. Some foods that are just "blah" are bursting with calories and fat- so make sure the food is worth the calories (is it tasty enough?). Educate yourself on what you put in your mouth! With the internet it is so easy to look up restaurants or at home look on packages and check the calories (remember fat free is not calorie free). Below is an example of how a simple drink can hide as many calories as a delicious (even junk food) meal:

An XL Pepsi from Taco Bell has 500 calories! You can drink a boring Pepsi OR For the same amount of calories you can have:

Large fries from McDonalds or a 7 Layer Taco Bell Burrito or 4 beef tacos from Del Taco or 4 English muffins with jelly add 40 more calories and you can even have a Big Mac!

Crazy to think a soda is the same as a meal! Why drink a real soda with all those calories when you can have water or a Diet soda for ZERO calories?? If you do not like Diet soda try filling your drink 90% Diet and just add real soda for the last 10% you will be surprised to see your whole soda tastes like real soda!

Just like we can make lifestyle changes with "moving" we can do that with food! You can still have a bean burrito just hold the cheese sometimes or devour those yummy fries with mustard instead of ranch. Add vegetables to your life! Try almonds instead of chips or fruit over gummy bears… Do not eliminate your favorite foods just have them in moderation.

Confront your problems and emotions with your mind NOT food! Sometimes we allow food to fill voids; we eat because we are sad, frustrated or even bored. Unfortunately good comfort food cannot solve our problems- sadly that is a fact! Sometimes over indulging on food can even make us feel worse afterwards- ugh. So find healthy ways to deal with your emotions. If you are angry it is amazing how an intense work out can make you feel better; release some of that steam through running or boxing! Or write out your emotions or lose yourself in a book or talking with a good friend.

Do not eat just to eat! Think about what you are eating and actually enjoy it and STOP when you are full. Eat slowly. If you want to lose weight, you can research how many calories you should be consuming a day. This will give you a gauge as to what is a good number. Remember that everyone is different so do not solely base anything on what someone else says- just do some research to get an idea of what works for you. So, once you know about food, you can decide if that large soda is worth the 500 calories or if you would rather spend that elsewhere. Some people will feel fabulous at 1,600 calories a day and others may need more or even less- it all depends on you (your height, weight and body type).

DO NOT STARVE YOURSELF! Starving yourself is the worst diet plan ever! It will make you moody, weak and quite miserable to be around. Depriving yourself of food or even treats is more likely to make you splurge and just give up. Starving yourself can damage your metabolism and make it harder in the future for you to maintain your weight. Skipping meals actually makes your body store fat! So the best route is to eat when you are hungry and eat small meals throughout the day.

No eating disorders! Throwing up your meals or starving yourself will just cause major problems (health, appearance, sanity and happiness). Diet pills will mess up your emotions, metabolism and have other serious side effects. Bulimia will destroy your insides including your teeth! These things can also all kill you! So gain control of your body and health the easy way through watching what you eat and exercising.

GOAL is to find a healthy balance! You cannot live your life on a diet! If you love food, eat the food you love JUST do it in moderation. Educate yourself on what you allow in your body! Explore foods, sports and exercises- you might find yourself loving things that are great for you! Exercise releases endorphins (they make us feel happy) so get out there and move and be your best happy self!

When You Call Me Ugly

When you call me ugly,
I know I am beautiful just the way I am.
You think I'm a slut.
Go ahead,
say it all you want.
As long as I know I'm a beautiful girl,
who knows who she really is,
deep inside.

Opinion Piece on Teen Pregnancy

There are a lot of issues that are leading to teens having babies. Some of these issues are because teens do not have an adult to talk to, do not know the consequences of sex, have a bad home situation/worry about family issues, and reality shows glorifying teen problems. It is easy to say we need to change. How do we make the changes needed to avoid teenage pregnancies?

A lot of teens have sex early because they do not have an adult they trust or feel comfortable talking with about sex. Many teens feel like their questions are simply not important to their parents or that their parents don't care. Teens do not feel comfortable, do not trust their parents, or are scared to disappoint the people around them, and they ultimately resort to their friends to learn about sex. What happens when friends do not give the right advice? Premature, uninformed sex, teen pregnancy, STDs, AIDs and HIV happen. Friends can also turn on you depending on who you had sex with, the timing, or the manner. So why do teens feel they can't go to their parents for help? Sometimes parents act weird about the subject of sex and that makes teens uncomfortable. What do teens want? Teens need/want a stable source of advice. The bottom line: sex is something we should talk about without feeling awkward.

Teens do know the consequences that may come with sex, but most of the time they live in "the moment." Girls and guys have sex before they are taught how to have "safe sex." Why is that? Do they have parents that treat them like they are already grown up? Or do they use sex to deal with problems they are going through?

Teens can get caught up with the problems of life and don't think about the consequences of their actions or choose to overlook what they are doing because sex feels good. Teens also want to experiment and discover things they don't really know about; they are curious. Being curious and experimenting with sex especially if teens are taking advice from other teens, results in them thinking "it can't happen to me." Teens have the mistaken idea that because it hasn't immediately happened to their friends, they cannot get pregnant or end up with a sexually transmitted disease. What teens don't realize is that having sex, especially "unsafe sex," can lead to teen pregnancy, sexually transmitted diseases, and orphaned children. Teens don't care about the facts before they "do it," again showing us that education at home is necessary to help prevent uninformed, premature teen sex.

Another thing to consider with teen pregnancy is the situation at home with boundaries and restrictions. Teenage pregnancy can result in teens living with strict rules and wanting to break from them or living with no rules or consequences. Teens do not set boundaries for themselves because they are not taught right from wrong at home or just choose to ignore it all. When parents worry more about work, bills, and marital problems, they forget the emotional needs of their children. Parents overlook teen issues when they are too distracted with work and school, and don't spend enough time with their families. The problem with parents today is that they communicate their frustrations, money problems, and marital issues to their children. Many teens feel the intense pressure trying to take their parents' role with their brothers and sisters and they figure they too can be parents, so why not? Most teen girls seek attention from guys and other friends because they do not get enough attention at home, which ends up in them not respecting themselves and giving in to peer pressure to fit in. the situation at home sets the boundaries for teens in the outside world, good or bad. So talk to us and let us know how to deal with it before we ask our friends or watch it on TV.

Reality shows on TV have been a platform for teen issues recently. With shows glorifying drinking, sex, drugs and pregnancy, teens learn to imitate and not to avoid these issues. Teens believe that whatever is on TV is cool which means having sex and getting pregnant is okay because of reality shows about teen moms. Teens don't realize that those teen moms are getting paid for being on TV so they take the GED to get out of school early. It is easier for them to take care of their kids with the money they make. TV, billboards and radio shows that star teen moms destroy the thinking of other teens. Teens getting paid for being a teen mom, can it happen? Yes. Will it happen to every teen mom? No. What the teen mom shows do tell teens is that most of the time teen fathers don't stick around for the kids. They also show that parents need to be in their teenager's life and know their friends. Teens learn that it is hard trying to go to prom and school when being pregnant.

The point in this opinion piece is that teens will do, experiment, and learn. Why not make it easier by sitting down and talking to us about safe sex, sexually transmitted diseases, pregnancy and prevention? Telling us "don't do it" hasn't made a difference, don't you think we need changes?

Strawberry Someone

I noticed that the strawberry has different
shades of red. It looks like the seeds
are eyes and the hair on the seed are eyelashes.
The green stem leaves look like hair.
It reminds me of someone's face.

Scar

On my arm, there formed a scar,
to keep me from birthing near or far,
in future, if month, or day and night
no more babies until the time is right.

Lungs

Why do they push me in a hole and not let me come up? Do they
want me to suffer? Do they want me to fear?

They throw me a shovel and say dig deeper. I dig and dig until
water fills my hole. All they say is keep digging, I do.

It's hard to breathe, keep digging, I do. My face is brown and my
lungs are weak as I take my last breath…..keep digging.

Body Scar

I have a scar that
I will cherish for
the rest of my life.

I never knew how amazing
a human body can be. Or
the life it can create...
Till I had my daughter
December 19, 2011, 9:56am.

I woke up with a 4 inch
cut on my stomach from
a C-section. The pain
or scar didn't bother
me, because it's something
I will have for the rest
of my life whether I'm
live or gone.

That's the thing about myself I haven't or
won't complain about. I gave birth to my
Beautiful, Healthy,

Smart, Nice

Baby Girl
Lyric La Niyah Morgan

Letter to Cancer Survivor

Hey Sweetie,

I am 14 years old and a high school freshmen in the ninth grade. My favorite color is rainbow. I love music and my friends. I just wanted to say "hi" and I know things are hard right now, but just keep your head up. Things are gonna get better. You have so many people who love and care about you. You wanna know a secret? My best friend had cancer last year and she had a brain tumor. Everyone thought they were gonna lose her. But guess what? She's still alive! She's a very important person in my life. I can't imagine my life without her. I'm sure your friends and family feel the same. Never lose hope. You're strong and you're gonna make it. If you ever want to talk, you can write me back.

Xoxo,

Always Here For You

VI

YOUR ANTI-DRUG

Perceptions &

Making the

Right Choices

My Story

My life is my story,

My story is me.

No one believes my story.

It is hidden.

The drugs I used,

The weed I smoked,

All made my story true.

This kid I have, he is so sweet and true.

But because of you, he's just like you.

Wish the best for him

Not to be like you.

He's my story, and it's true.

He's just like you.

Unconscious

How would you like to be in my shoes
Where people call you crazy
And say you have issues
All they do is label and criticize
And they don't take time out
To see the hurt in your eyes
Growing up labeled as a problem child
Mom's on drugs and dad has gone wild
Taking in so much
But not letting anything go
Because you're too afraid
To let your feelings show.
One night you get high as the sky
To feel the feeling you feel best
Your alcohol on the table
And the weed on the nightstand
Some guy is in your face
Asking questions you can't answer
You gag and cough
Like you have lung cancer
You see yourself
But it's not you
Your mom is saying if she only knew
You wake up and scream
And start to pray
Thanking the lord
For another day.

Life

Life we perceive life as a
Problem for the majority of us.
We don't know why it's hard
And we don't know why it's built up with scars.
We eventually get tired of all the negativity,
So we find ways to keep busy.
The problem was we don't know how
Far ahead we can get so we stop and break.
And we turn to the one who gave us life.
We start to think, pray for the things we need and they come
sooner than you think.

True Friendship

I love you,
but you love drugs
more than you love me.
I'm your friend.
I care and love you.
Drugs don't care or love you.
I'm your friend
and I can't kill you,
but drugs can.

Effects of Drugs

It's important to know facts about drugs you are thinking about using. You also have to understand the risk you are taking when using the drugs. Some feel confused and pressured about taking drugs. When you are making a decision whether you want to take the drugs or not, think about these following points:

1. Do you really know what you're taking?

2. Do you know about the person who is selling it to you?

3. How likely is it that you will have a positive experience?

4. Can you really afford to?

5. Do you know what the risks are and what to do if something goes wrong?

If you're taking drugs, it is possible to believe that you can handle the effects of the drugs you are using. Taking drugs might make you feel good but there are consequences to taking that drug. These are five things affected by drugs.

1. Your speed

2. Attention

3. Flexibility

4. Problem solving

5. Memory

Heroin is made to cure people of addiction to morphine. Morphine is a pain reliever that treats moderate to severe pain. Heroin is converted into morphine. This creates a sense of well-being. The characteristic euphoria has been described as an "orgasm centered in the gut." Heroin makes you feel like doing things fast, in a rush, and it also makes you very nervous.

Cocaine is a crystalline tropane alkaloid that comes from leaves of the coca plant. Cocaine has been described as a séance of happiness and increased energy. The cocaine can last up to 20 hours depending on the dosage of cocaine. Cocaine increases blood pressure, increases heart rate and euphoria. Euphoria is sometimes followed by feelings of comfort and also depression and the craving of using cocaine again. Cocaine also has side effects that can include twitching, paranoia and impotence. Paranoia means someone distrusts people.

In conclusion, drugs have serious side-effects, can impair judgment and even lead to addiction or death. They can hurt relationships and affect the way we behave or how our minds develop. It's worth educating yourself, knowing the risks, and talking to an adult you trust about about the risks of drugs. And it's important to ask for help if you're having a hard time staying away from drugs.

Are They For You?

Drugs - are they for you?
Do you think you can make it through?
If you think you can make it through,
If you say not, I say no too.

If I were to ask you,
Could you smoke a joint or two?
What would you say?

Would you realize and come through?
Or would you say yes and realize it's not true?
Think about it.
Are drugs for you?

Senses

This strawberry looks oh so yummy, it's bright red color, red as
blood, it's nice dark green leaves as green as healthy grass.
Sometimes I sit and wonder how it has so many tiny holes with
seeds in them all perfectly aligned as if someone themselves
designed it. The seeds look like freckles on a kid's face, when you
take that first bite it fills your mouth with pure sweetness and it
drives your taste buds crazy and asking for more.

Release

I want to release my past, the drugs, the hate.

I want to release my heart from that pain.

 I want to release the images of my past do they no longer exist.

I want to release all my childhood memories so they no longer last.

I release myself to be the person I am today. For not being caught in my family's daze.

I release myself to my future.

Always Remembered, Never Forgotten

He passed away Friday morning. His death took us by surprise.
Never again will we see his smile or look into his eyes. His body
is cold, yet his hands are warm. His eyes just stare and you realize
he is gone. His dad is in the room. He feels alone. Knowing that
out of two boys, one will not come home. Two days later, his
dad's still in shock, living with unbearable pain. Even when the
sun shines, all he sees is rain. The tears echo in our hearts, because
it seems he was too young. Everyone agrees. Because Dustin was
only 19.

Family,

I am writing this to you all to explain my actions and what I feel and do to myself. I know that I have been distant and different. It's most of you know, although I still hid it; I am a drug addict. And yet, I still try to hide it. I know you all may think you know what goes through my mind when I do the drugs, but would you ever believe that I don't think or feel anything because I don't want to. I take the drugs to numb the pain. I come home faded from weed. When I'm not on the substance, I walk into my father screaming or hitting my mom, sisters with big mouths and dirty looks. They all turn on me to relieve their pain, so I run to my room trying hard to fight the tears. I grab the pipe, needle, or the snow white. Filing my life with these substances help me undo my wrongs or their wrongs. Sometimes I say I take the drugs because of my horrid family, my idiot friends, or even my enemies. I place blame on everyone but myself, because I feel nothing for those who make my life imperfect. I don't trust anyone or anything but the drugs because I take the cocaine, heroin, or weed to calm my life own from them. If they truly cared, they wouldn't hurt me and help me stop using the substances. Although you all thought it was my mind and my stupid teen years, but just so you know: it's my life and who's in it.

-Your lost drug-addict son

Phone Call to the Drug-Hotline

Ring…ring... the phone rings.
I picked up and it was Emily.
She said, "Hello, Nancy, how are you?"

"Hello, Emily, I am grateful to see you," I replied.
"Well, I'm not so good. I'm addicted to amphetamine and I need your advice and help."

"Really…dang, Emily!" I exclaimed.
"I don't know what to say. I can't believe you would do something like that," I said, feeling sad.

"Yes, Nancy, it's all me. I thought I was so fat, so I wanted to go the easy way. Please don't judge me, Nancy."

"Oh, I won't, Emily. I'm your friend. I would like to help you recover, but you know that there are possibilities that you can get addicted to amphetamine. Didn't you know my dad lost his family because he did amphetamines? He went crazy. One day late at night he came home with a bloody knife saying that he just sliced some black man's throat. Now he hears voices. He is still recovering."

"Wow. Really?"

"Yes, Emily. It's no joke playing with the devil."

"What do you mean?"

"I mean that the amphetamine piece is the devil."

"Well, what should I do, Nancy?"

"Well, I can't help you, but Alateen can."

"What's Alateen?"

"It's a program where they help you recover from addiction. So, you have a choice: to get help or die from the addiction. You can only help yourself. You are only stronger if you do things the right way. You know that once you were going to use amphetamine, there was a possibility that you could get addicted to it. You know what's right and wrong, go to Alateen and get help!"

Stop the Drugs

Drugs.

Let it go.

Be free.

Stay healthy.

Think of the future.

Forget the past.

Eat veggies.

Play with your teddy bear.

Don't do drugs.

Live your life.

Be happy.

Be healthy.

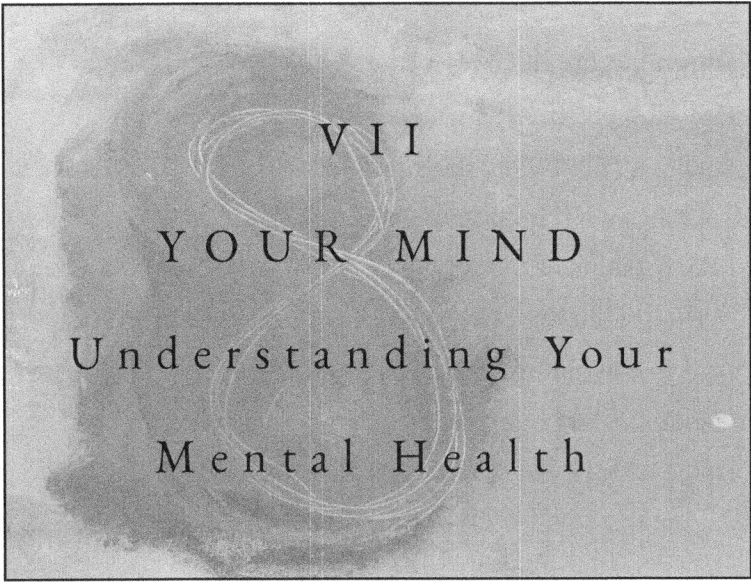

VII

YOUR MIND

Understanding Your

Mental Health

Riding the Waves

Our minds are like the ocean,
Bringing unexpected water
And the calm before the storm.
Together we'll try & navigate
Like captains of the sea,
Surfers riding the waves,
And fish avoiding predators.
Understanding our minds
Helps us save our sandcastles from the tide,
And prepare us for the storm.

Pockets

The pockets of my life
are filled with happiness.
Deep down I know
I am loved.
I want to explain
my depression.

Lost

When I look up in the sky
I see birds and trees.
I wish I would see the real me.
When I look in the mirror
I see eyes staring back at me.
I wonder who can that be.
When I look at you
I wonder do I have to be like that too.
When I look down to the ground
I wonder will I ever be found?

Learn

Learn you are beautiful
Learn that you have so much to offer
Learn that problems are temporary
Learn who you are
Learn to not care what people think of you
Learn that they would judge you anyway
Learn that life is short
Learn happiness is a state of mind

Release

Sadness from anger I want to release
Tears and worry fill me. So much I want, so much I have.
I will one day soon take my tears and worry to release.
No more.
It's released.

Scarring Moments

I have a scar that is visible
I hide it from most
Because I don't want to be judged for it
Because others like it
This scar has so many memories of questions
And thoughts on this scar I made it to remind me
Of that day for that day but it has stuck with me for years after
That one bad day
I am ashamed of this scar and the others like it
But they all served their purpose
At there time to take the pain on the inside
Out to the outside and not let me
Focus on my emotional pain I felt at the moment
I made these scars

Open Letter on Self Injury (Cutting)

Dear Sissy,

It makes me very sad to know that you're unhappy. I know
growing up the way we did wasn't easy, especially for you being
the oldest. You had a lot more responsibilities and pressures put on
by mom and dad; And that made you stressed. I wish you could
help me understand why you would intentionally hurt yourself the
way you do. I can't imagine why someone would cut themselves as
a way to relieve pressure. I look at your forearms and many
horizontal scars that are white and faded. I honestly couldn't
imagine feeling so stressed that I have to inflict pain on myself.
Having enough strength to cut my skin with a razor blade and then
feeling better. We both grew up in the same conditions, so I
sometimes can't understand why you would do such a thing. I
guess we have different ways of dealing with our emotions. I hope
someday you will stop cutting yourself, and realize there are other
ways to deal with stress and pressure that you feel. I hope you take
yourself out of the environment you are in, and find better people
to surround yourself with. Cutting is a serious mental health
problem, and if you don't get help you might accidentally do
something you can't take back. I know we don't have the best
relationship but I hope you take this letter into consideration. So
someday we can have the relationship that we always wanted.

Love,

Hope

Safehaven

I feel safe in this room I built in my mind.
It has a window that I can look out
It has a very comfortable, cozy chair
It has a door with a lock on it
It is clean and serene
It is quite and peaceful.

This room is my safe haven in my mind
That no one can hurt me
No one can find me
This place is safe

Second Chances

A young girl lost her child to social services because she was depressed, had suicidal ideations and ended up in the mental institution. Does she deserve a second chance to raise her child? Every human being has made a mistake in her life and wanted to "re-do" the past. Most people have received that second chance; and the young woman who lost her child should also be afforded that same chance. Making a mistake in life sometimes helps a person get better and build character. Everybody deserves a second chance including that young woman. Some people may disagree, believing she does not deserve that chance. They will say she will not be responsible enough. Some will think if she had a mental breakdown, she is not stable enough to take care of her child.

The impact of parental mental illness on family life and children's well-being can be significant. Children whose parents have a mental illness are at risk of developing social, emotional and/or behavioral problems. But, even those parents can fix their problem. If the parent follows the court's orders, shows stability, responsibility and the willingness to be the person their child needs and deserves, they should be given a second chance. Everybody in this world has made a mistake and wanted to fix it. Some of us deserve a second chance.

Just Like You

I am the face of disgrace while you are a beautiful lace. So perfect, so clean, so purity.

Fresh out of the package, no rips it seems, not even a splash of ink.

Now look at me. I am ripped and torn in more directions than one – beyond torn.

Pieces missing not even tape can fix.

I used to be just like you, the one everyone wanted to use.

Now they crumple me up and throw me away until next trash day.

It's Time Now

I am releasing you, my pets. I am loosening the leash for you to run, but not too far I pray.

I still need you. Don't go fully away.

Anger, my pet. Fear, my pet. I'm letting you go. I release my firm grip.

I raised you. I let you grow. You are fully matured.

Now you must go.

A Cover Up

I will mask it. I will cover it up. It will have never existed as if thrown up.

I'll paint the walls. Change the color. Make things brighter as if lighting a bonfire.

I will wash my face. Remove dew from my eyes. Powder my cheeks and apply mascara to homely eyes.

I will walk the halls, a normal day, and everyone will think I'm okay.

Open Letter from Perpetrator to Victims

Dear Scared Victims,

Well, I ended up winning the thing you call battle, but for me, this was me against the world. People think that it's so easy, that we or I am just some crazy person. Sometimes that's the case but most of the time it's a dramatic event or a personality that got you like this. Before you judge me for what I've done or who I am, trust me when I say, I have a mind you don't want to understand. I am not crazy or a freak. I have reasons and that's why I'm writing this. I want you to understand why I did what I did from my perspective of life. Things aren't sky blue, it's a tragedy and I wanted you to pay, feel the pain I felt when you threw me around, messed with me and all those other things that I couldn't take anymore. I exploded…my revenge wasn't as I planned, I had a little too much fun. I actually enjoyed watching you bleed to death…I was the last thing you saw and the last thing you'll ever see because..well, nana, we're both going to hell! I just want you to know one last thing, you won the battle but you lost the war.

Signed,

Disturbed

Open Letter from Child Victim of Suicide to Mother

Dear Mom,

I know you blame yourself, but you did nothing wrong...the reason I committed suicide was the mean girls at my school. They pushed me around, called me names, spread rumors about me and did more than you can imagine. So, I decided on suicide. The girls have been doing this for the whole school year. I was watching a movie once and the star overdosed on medical pills, so I did the same. It seemed like the easiest and least painful way to do it. So I went to your bathroom, opened your medicine cabinet, took out your headache pills and took the five pills that were left. After that, I put on my most pretty dress and put my hair back in a bun and lay in my bed. While I laid in my bed, I thought of all my family members and friends. I knew what I was doing. I knew the consequences of my actions. So, I just want to say, I love you. Just tell the mean girls at my school, I just wanted to be your friend.

Signed,

Forever Alone

Open Letters from Friend to Victim of Bullying

Dear Beautiful,

You're not alone in this cold world! There are people who care. You just have to see past those people that don't matter. Trust me, I was there also where I felt unwanted, like I didn't matter to anyone, like if I died no one would stop to question "Where is she?" But now I see that people do care. You just have to get out there, meet new people and join groups. Yeah, I know that is gonna be hard but hey, nothing's ever easy in life. But that doesn't mean you should give up because honestly I don't know what I would do without you. You're my best friend, even though you don't notice. I saw those scars on your wrist. You're not only hurting yourself, you're hurting me also. Do I not matter enough for you to continue living? So, please think twice before you try to do anything dumb this time. Luckily, your mom was there to stop you. You just have to always remember that everyday holds a new dawn, yesterday is already behind you and it's up to you to make today better because if no one can take away our sadness, why would you ever let anyone take away your happiness? I understand that you have problems of your own, but there are people that have it a million times worse. They're still trying their hardest to survive. If they can do it, why can't you? I know you're strong and smart. I mean, you're only fifteen and literally have your whole life ahead of you. Two more years and we will be off to college and those people that are putting you down right now won't matter because they will be working at Carl's Jr. or McDonald's while we're off in Chicago. So, please don't leave me here by myself. I need you. Your mom needs you! Please don't throw all your dreams away because of these stupid people that have nothing better to do than spit out junk at the people that they know are better than them. Just remember that I love you and that you do matter way more than you think.

With lots of love,

Sunny

Dear Hopeless,

I understand that you have problems of your own, but there are people that have it a million times worse, and they are still trying their hardest to survive. If they can do it, why can't you?

I know you are strong and smart. I mean you are only 15. You literally have your whole life ahead of you.

Two more years and we will be off to college, and those people that are putting you down right now won't matter. They will be working at Carl's Jr. or McDonald's, while we are off in Chicago.

So, please don't leave me here by myself. I need you. Your mom needs you. Please don't throw all your dreams away because of these stupid people that have nothing better to do than spit out their shit at the people that they know are better than them. Just remember that I love you, and that you do matter way more than you think.

Here for you,

Your Hopeful Friend

VIII

YOUR SPIRIT

Making Your

Heart Dance

Home

Home is a place I enjoy being
Not literally where I fall asleep every night and wake up every
morning
Home is a place where I'm surrounded by people I love and love
me in return
Not a house or a bed
Home is where I can be myself
Not feeling alone

A Safe Place

I feel safe with one person. I feel safe in one place.
Person and place, all in one.
Person and place, all the same.
Loved and cherished, conversation and fun.

Berry Happy

The strawberry reminds me of getting strawberries from my grandma's house. They are so delicious to eat. It is so refreshing when I eat them. It makes me feel happy inside.

It also comes from the ground and is healthy for you. I like strawberries because you can dip them in white chocolate or milk chocolate or a fountain that has the chocolate running down the strawberry.

My Eyeballs

These eyes aren't ordinary eyes. They are my eyes. I love how they change from color to color; sometimes there are even three colors at once.

These eyes see a lot of things whether it is good or bad.

Whether I should have seen it or not. They see things people didn't think they had seen.

These eyes aren't always happy and you can tell by just looking at them. You can look deep into these eyes and answer questions yourself without the help of my mouth to respond.

These eyes will always glow no matter what the situation. These eyes are my eyes and that's how it's going to be until my heart stops and I take my last breath.

That Food

Watching my mom bake a cake, her short figure reaches for the flour in the cabinet, like a ballerina on her tippy toes. She gathers up all the other ingredients needed as well, then pours the batter out into a pan and sticks it in the oven.

After a few minutes the aroma of the cakes fills up the whole house.

I love the way my mom cooks, the big 'ol colgate smile on her face as if she can do it forever.

I Am

I am from a place surrounded by flowers. Nature is the one thing I enjoy, from watching flowers bloom, bees buzzing and humming birds flying; picking fruit off the trees.

Making homemade orange juice, the aroma of freshness in the air as if someone sprayed Febreze, watching my siblings run around and laughing. Laughing so much my stomach hurts as if I've just been sucker-punched.

The big tall trees with branches that look like arms reaching out to you.

The smell of Mexican food fills my nose and the smell of chili tingles my senses.

The Beach

I am the beach,

I have lots of water.

The beautiful horizon shines over the water,

a reflection for you to see.

I never grow old.

The world comes during the summer to see me.

The camera you use to take pictures of me,

will bring memories that will last forever, that over the

generations will get to see.

Your family, they'll come along to visit me,

making more and more memories of the beautiful sea.

A Funny Moment

On a hot, sunny day on a Saturday I went over to the yard sale people. They always gave us free stuff, so they gave us a big bucket full of stuff. My family went through it and everyone got some stuff.

Then I put on this pair of shirts and my brother was right behind me. My brother has short, brown hair with blond in it. He is so tall, and he has big feet. He is a really nice brother. So I put on the shirts and my brother was right behind me, so when I went to take them off, I pulled my pants off with them.

My brother said nothing. I think I scarred him for life. My face was red like a cherry. I never thought that would happen to me in my life. My family laughed at me for so long. That was the joke of the day.

Starview

My life is so messed up in Starview.
I have to share a shower and a restroom with five other girls.
And my bed, I can imagine where my peers have been.

I pray to the Lord I make it through the next day,
and to give me salvation.
In the end, we don't belong here.
We are wonderful in our own ways.
I pray to the Lord that he saves us from whatever it is we go
through.

To Feel

To feel bad but good
Loved but not
Peace is in me
I can't show the real me
To be afraid of life
To put on a smile
To please everyone but me
To live a life you know you don't want
To live
To feel pain that is not good
To find someone that is good to me
To feel gone when you live

IX
YOUR STYLE
Creating Your Own

Inside Out

It don't matter how I look or dress,

The beauty is not on the outside,

but the true beauty is on the inside.

I may dress crappy and not wear makeup,

but I'm beautiful in my own way.

I may not be skinny and pretty,

but I'm beautiful inside.

I may not be the perfect girl, or like the other girls,

But I'm beautiful inside.

I may have scars and be quiet,

but I'm beautiful inside.

A lot of things can be ugly and indifferent on the outside,

But the true beauty is on the inside.

Hair

My hair is what I hide behind when I am nervous. It is what I hide
behind when I don't want to be bothered. And it is what I hide
behind in the early mornings when I do not look my best.
Hair is what I use to express myself and what I use to tell you
about myself. I feel my best when my long dark curly hair is down
and frizzy and I don't really care enough to do much with it
because I have more important things on my mind. When my hair
is pulled back into a tight messy bun is when I feel my worst.
When I can't bear to feel anything my face, back, or shoulders.

My Hair

My hair is long and curly.
It doesn't have lice so don't you worry.
My hair blows in the wind,
and is furry when I put it up.
It does what it wants,
either shape or size.
It doesn't matter, it likes it's own style.
It's happy when it's down.
My hair might not go to the ground,
but I make sure it looks beautiful
when people are around.
It always looks cool
when I waive it in the wind.

Made Up Mess

My hair is a nappy big piece of mess.
I always throw it up in a bun.
There's no reason to dress up,
or ever to look my best.
I think I look horrible.
My hair, my clothes -- I don't even bother.
Maybe I should.
Maybe one day I could.

My Hair

My hair is long and curly.
It doesn't have life, so don't you worry.
My hair blows in the wind.
It does what it wants.
Shape or size doesn't matter.
It likes its own style.
It's happy when it's down.
My hair might not go to the ground,
but it sure looks beautiful
when people are around.
It is always cool
when you wave it in the wind.

Beautiful Future Self

She's beautiful with long, light brown hair, slightly messy, with locks of curls flowing down. The strikingly beautiful white dress kisses the ground. I seek the depth of her eyes and see the kind, beautiful golden brown eyes.

With flawless looks, she shows a dazzling smile! She whispers and gently touches my palms with her soft, warm hands. She tells me to believe within myself - to know I have the ability to change, keep my head up, never show my fear of life, and embrace the chance of change it offers.

Inside Beauty

It doesn't matter how I look or dress.
The beauty is not on the outside,
but the true beauty is in the inside.
I may dress poorly and not wear makeup,
but I'm beautiful in my own way.
I may not be skinny and pretty,
but I'm beautiful inside.
I may not be the perfect girl
or like the other girls,
but I'm beautiful inside.
I may have scars and be quiet,
but I'm beautiful inside.
A lot of things can be ugly and
indifferent on the outside.
But the true beauty is in the inside.

Mayonesa Hair

To me, my hair is my life. In the past, I needed to wear extensions,
because my hair was too short. My Nana would tell me, "Mija,
your hair is beautiful." So that day I tore my extensions.
My nana told me my hair will grow, if I put mayonesa in it.
As time went on, it did. I love my hair. It takes a long time to do,
but in the end it is all worth it.

Green Eyed

I appreciate my eyes.
They allow me to see
And are green like grass.

Colors

I like the colors Blue and Red!

Blue makes me happy and I can just be me

Red helps me to be cheerful when I'm sad

These colors show me who I can be.

They show me I can be a better person and successful person with well-defined goals.

Makeup

I think about fashion and my beauty needs.

So, make-up and cosmetics are some of my favorites.

I want to have a nice body and a college degree.

My Favorite Things

I like the color blue.

I love playing basketball.

My favorite NBA team is the Lakers.

My favorite food is pasta.

My favorite NFL team is the Chargers.

God loves me and you.

What I love

My life is about love, care, and hope.

I want to be a counselor, because I think

I have a voice for the people in need.

I feel I can help with problems.

I love candy, reading, writing, sparkles,

glitter, nail polish, and most of all – music.

My hobbies are crafts.

I decorate #2 pencils. It is really fun. I love it!

I hate being bored, and when people try

to be like other people who think they are cool.

I don't understand why no one can be real.

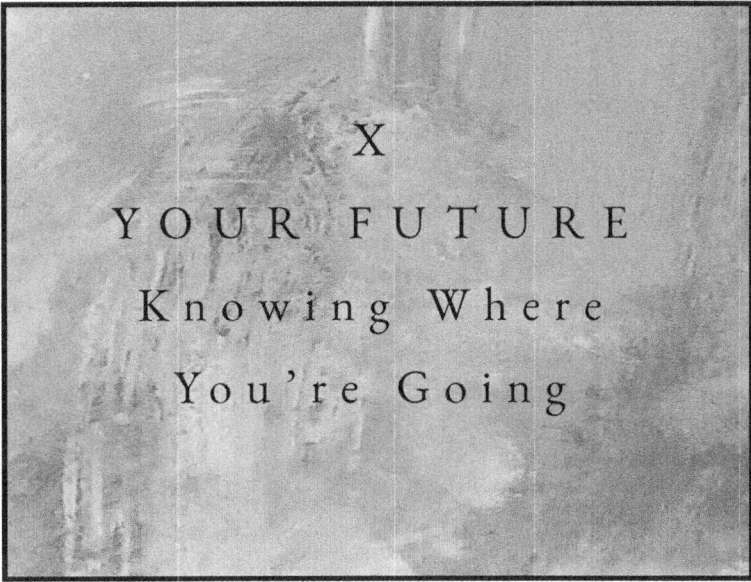

X

YOUR FUTURE

Knowing Where

You're Going

Follow Your Dreams.

The Women Wonder Writers Creed

Drop it. Let it go. Let the past be the past.

Despite it all, I will stand tall.

From this day forward,

I start a new journey.

I take a stand,

With pen in hand.

My words have power.

My words matter.

I matter.

I am a young scribe,

With a story of my own.

My open journal awaits.

I give myself permission to try.

I am creative.

I am adventurous.

I am original.

I am young.

Words are my greatest tool, my greatest weapon.

I will use them wisely,

I am a survivor and I will thrive.

My best future-self, wait no more, I am here.

The Woman Bottled up in Me

She is confidant, she isn't afraid to stand tall
and take her eyes away from her feet.
She isn't afraid of falling so she doesn't.
She's like a flower blooming so strong
and beautiful but she's so deep down
and out of reach I fear I won't find her.
My desire to be this person is so great
but my habit of wondering what everyone
is thinking of me is in my way.
If I let that go then maybe I could stand tall too.

Encouraging words

You are strong!
You can accomplish anything you set your mind to.
You are beautiful.
You are kind.
You will be happy!
Never give up.

My Self

My self tells me that I am going to be skinny and beautiful.

That I will be successful.

That I will grow up and have a life.

That I won't be depressed.

That I will be able to thankful for what I have in my life.

That I will move forward, have progress,

and achieve many things and goals

I set out for my life and my family.

The Ladies

Group of ladies
Walking at night
Causing trouble
Wanting to fight.

One of the ladies
Falling in love
Blind from the world
Using no glove.

No more ladies
Now a baby
Wants no more trouble
Wants to give the world to her baby.

But no more ladies
Wants the best for her little baby.

Learn

Learn you are beautiful.

Learn that you have so much to offer.

Learn that problems are temporary.

Learn who you are.

Learn to not care what people think of you.

Learn that they would judge you anyway.

Learn that life is short.

Learn happiness is a state of mind.

Learn

Learn to appreciate the life around you

Learn to never question your capabilities

Learn to get back up if you can while the struggle or without a doubt after it learn to have fun despite the reasons you feel you shouldn't be learn to be yourself and live proud of it Learn to be forgiving and understanding but most of all learn who you want to be

Learn how much your father loves you and how much your mother loved you too even if you feel your mother has abandon you

Learn to appreciate you got to meet her

Learn to love yourself and learn to appreciate even what you cannot see

I Will

My future self tells me that I'm going to be skinny and beautiful,
and that I will be successful.
That I won't be depressed.
I will be able to be thankful for what I have in my life.
And I will be able to move forward and have progress.
And that I will be able to achieve so many goals
that I set out there for my life and my family.

Father's Words

Learn the good in me not the bad but if you so happen to learn the
bad learn from it learn to stay on your toes
Learn to take care of yourself, you don't need a mans help
Learn to work hard for the things you want
Learn to stay happy
Learn to always get up and try again

You think you're a BULLY
until you lose yourself FULLY.
Quit pushing in the HALLWAY
and make your own PATHWAY.

Safe Places

Safe to me will have
to be Safe House TLP.

To know that I'm
somewhere with people that
help and support you to
guide you to be a
better person in life.

I'm safe because I
have a roof over my head,
clothes on my back, food
to eat, water to wash my
body, lights to see, a place
to call home.

I'm safe because I'm
somewhere I can leave
knowing I'm ok. I have
more knowledge then I
came here with.

My Parental Self

Each time I close my eyes and open them,
I am thankful for where I stand today.
Two years ago I was not who I am today.
I was following someone else but not myself.
Today I follow myself.
My parental self makes me realize that this change was good.
But most important, this change was for me and no one else.

To Better Myself

The only place I felt
safe at was my mom's
house because I didn't
have to worry about
drama and tomorrow's
worries, but all that
changed in 2008 when
she was taken from me;
she was all I had, and
now I'm in a position
I am trying to get myself out
of to better myself.

Strawberry

Even though it's not perfect

It's beautiful and useful.

Shows how much we take for granted.

A little strawberry, imperfections and all

Holds the potential to be so much greater.

All it needs is love, care, and the proper nutrients.

Just a chance – an opportunity.

Scars

You were made out of hurt and pain. You remind me happiness will always remain.

I should have thought twice before you were born – to learn better ways to cope and morn.

I was younger back then and yet you stay. Keeping me company everyday.

A daily reminder of what's been done. How I cried how I lied.

As long as you are with me, I'll never get lost on that path to rot and die.

Fly High

I am releasing my shyness. I am releasing you to many
opportunities I let fly away.

I am releasing you into the benign light where you belong.

I am releasing you for my own sake, for my own well-being.

You have overpowered me for many years but it's now time to fly
away.

If you dare come back, I promise you I will release you into the
dark obscurity so you don't fly your way back to me.

My family

Family is always here for me
No matter what.
Through the struggles in my life
They will always be here
To help me through everything.

Glow

Many things seem so bright.
But I burst out
In so many ways.
I could be painted, but
Not turn into gray.

In the Future

In the future, I want to complete High School

Afterwards, join the Navy and become an Orthopedic Doctor

In the future, I will be a wealthy lady with lots of money.

One Step at a Time

I want to be happy in future!

I am not happy now but I'm working through the hard days

One step at a time. I will surely get there

I know there will be bad days in the future too

But I want to have logical reasons to be upset in the future!

Purple

My favorite color is purple.

Why? I don't know.

I think it inspires me to do great things.

Great things like going back to school and getting a High School Diploma.

It inspires me to break barriers and go to Medical School

And become an Oncologist or Nursing School to become a Registered Nurse.

My future is Purple Bright!

Beautiful

I have random and beautiful thoughts.

I think about my family, best friend, music and food.

These beautiful things inspire me to look into the future with hope

I hope to see my kids grow up and meet their goals in life

My future will be beautiful!

My Own Steps

I want to become a better person

Not just for myself but for my family

I want to be a good influence for my little siblings and cousins

I don't want them to struggle like I did

I need to start focusing on what makes me happy and not others

I want to be a leader and not a follower

I don't want to follow!

I want to walk in my own steps!

To Serve

After High School, I want to join the Navy

I want to serve in the Navy for six years

I want to travel around the world

I want to study to become an Engineer in the Navy

I want to work on the sea.

A New Day

I rise every morning to see and know I survived another day,
Another day to thank God,
Thank God to let me see the morning light,
Morning light that brightens my day,
The day that will surprise me with something new to learn,
Something new I learned that will help me the next day.

Wild Life

They said monsters were under the bed
Monsters in dolls
Monsters behind doors
In our closet even
The monsters were everywhere.

But then I noticed the only monster in our rooms
Are inside of us.
Since the monsters aren't under the bed, but inside us,
I turned that bad monster into a good monster.

There is no bad or good monster itself,
but it's the one that we create and keep growing.

Fragile Flight

A little birdie once asked God
"God, will I be able to be free?"

"Yes, you will. But there are cages to open,
obstacles to pass, an egg to crack,
and wings to stretch."

The little birdie had cracked his egg that night.
He had gone through so many days in that cage of his,
until he finally opened it. Now he just had to avoid the danger,
so he can soon fly.

When the day came to soon fly, he opened his wings and
No longer than 30 seconds, he was soon free to fly.

A Fresh Beginning

Burnt, like I've been so many times. I am feeling the frustration rise within me.

Split, like when I've been torn away from my family and not to be seen for so long.

Died, like I had to hide my identity from the world and afraid to show the real me.

But it will be cut and new and layered, like the fresh beginning that I've been offered in life. Like the new personality I'm having grow inside.

Layered like the many steps I've had to take to get and be the person I am today. I will forget the past, but I will not forget what it has taught me.

Always give a helping hand to those in need.

Youth Letter to Ruth

Dear Ruth,

I am so glad I met you. I am glad that you write books. You do a good job expressing your feelings. I like how you're not sad about what you feel. You tell about how you can move on in your life and think of the positive, not the negative.

I think you are a wonderful person. I am so glad that you survived the Holocaust. I think you were very brave. I enjoyed meeting you.

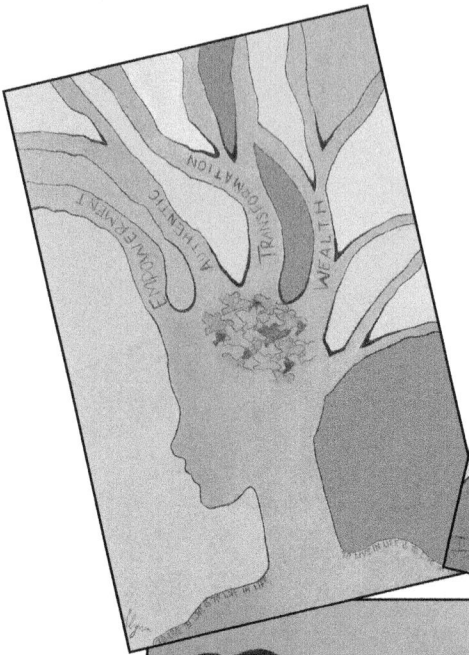

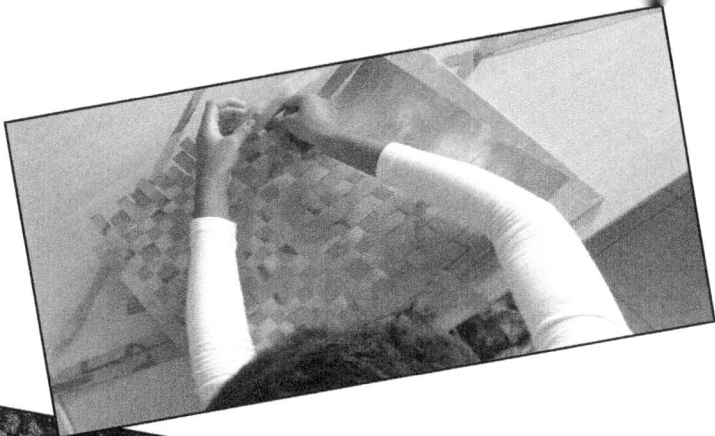

THE WRITE OF YOUR L!FE™

Ⓦ WomenWonderWriters

The youth who contributed to the *Perspectives* Anthology participated in *The Write of Your L!fe™*, a life skills and mentoring program created by Women Wonder Writers™ (WWW). WWW is a 501(c)(3) nonprofit organization whose mission is to break the cycle of victimization and transform the criminal justice system. WWW accomplishes this by implementing creative intervention and mentorship programs for at-risk youth affected by abuse, crime, broken homes or who are underachieving academically and by teaching them accountability, empathy and self-expression through art, writing and public speaking. WWW believes that no matter one's past or hardships, resilience is possible.

WWW welcomes your support and participation; visit WWW at WomenWonderWriters.com.

Made in the USA
Las Vegas, NV
22 September 2021